'I see you'
are
three words
that separate

As if the one who sees
is not the same as the one
who is seen

Acknowledge the image,
a clear view,
of how this person
appears to others

And also to this "me".

The woman in the mirror
wishes to do what she does

With more honesty
And more potential
And more curiosity
And more skill

I see her say
I am seeing
the truth

I say she sees
the truth
I am saying

I see the truth
she sees, saying
I AM

Jane Hardjono

FACILITATING
REFLECTIONS

Published by: Thomas Lahnthaler AS
www.lahnthaler.com

First Edition 2025

Illustrations by Hannah Grønvold
Graphs by Stefanie Wiener
Book design by Wolf Wiener
Handwritten notes by the author

ISBN 978-1-7396286-3-5 (paperback)
ISBN 978-1-7396286-2-8 (ebook)

FACILITATING
REFLECTIONS

Thomas Lahnthaler

In memory of my mother

The first facilitator I ever knew.
A teacher in your unique ways.
All that remains is gratitude.

BEFORE YOU DIP OR DIVE INTO
THE BOOK, FIND A MIRROR.
(OR YOUR PHONE WILL
DO JUST FINE.)

COMMIT TO FOLLOWING
THE PROCESS THIS BOOK REPRESENTS,
WHEREVER IT TAKES YOU.
ACKNOWLEDGE WHATEVER IT
DOES OR DOESN'T TRIGGER IN YOU
AND THOROUGHLY EXPLORE
THE SOURCE OF THESE REACTIONS.

SAY THIS IN YOUR OWN WORDS
AS YOU WITNESS YOURSELF
SAYING THEM ALOUD.

THANK YOU!

TAKE A MOMENT TO REFLECT
ON WHAT HAS COME TO THE
SURFACE ALREADY.

FEEL FREE TO USE THE SPACE
BELOW OR ANY OTHER JOURNAL
IF YOU WANT TO TAKE NOTES.

WELCOME TO FACILITATING REFLECTIONS

Arrogant. Condescending. Self-centred. Pretentious. Exclusive. God complex.

These would be harsh enough judgments on their own, but they are even more hurtful in context. I heard these words in conversations with professionals from various sectors about their views on facilitators and facilitation. Hard to not take personally as my work has involved being a facilitator for almost 20 years.

Zooming out, I started to see why they saw facilitators and, consequently, facilitation this way. I've now been inside and outside "the bubble," and I too detect an air of exclusivity (that morphs into a small whirlwind the closer you get). From the outside it sure does seem to be all about the fanciest framework, the most exciting method. How facilitators hold space, and know all about psychological safety and empathy. They're the ones with the most amazing questions, are constantly having fun, create meaningful experiences, and will solve any conflict!

Okay. My practice is heavily influenced by my time with Indigenous communities, in war zones, and crisis contexts. For me, facilitation is one of the most human crafts there is. So when I engaged in these chats within the facilitator community itself, I felt increasingly distant from the entire conversation. It seemed like a never-ending wheel of mutual re-affirmation.

This prompted me to engage in my favorite activity: observing, listening, and learning. And what I sensed was a disconnect.

And one day it struck me.

Facilitation is in desperate need of a <u>YARN</u>.

I was introduced to this First Nation Australian term many years ago when I spent weeks with them in a sacred ritual on Elcho Island. Yarning is one of the most beautiful and enriching concepts.

Simplified, to 'yarn' is to have a conversation where right and wrong are irrelevant concepts. It exchanges views, thoughts, realizations, beliefs, and ideas. It is an invitation to share without having to convince, agree, or find the ultimate truth. It is a journey of discovering different views. It doesn't feed on questions but rather, on observing, listening, and learning. Every contribution is an add-on to the previous one, expanding the collective reality on the topic.

But to do that, we must be aware of who we are, what we think, and why we believe it. If we don't, a yarn can become an overwhelming experience where we get lost in a sea of views, desperately needing answers that we didn't know we already had inside us.

This is the core of this book. It is an invitation to yarn — a yarn with yourself.

This book doesn't follow a linear process, it's circular. It doesn't have a beginning or an end, and if you try to find one, it will slip between your fingers and you might find another beginning or end somewhere else. You can give it a linear go and read/do it from the first page to the last, or you can open it wherever you like and start from there. You are in control of where, when (and whether) you want to start.

You'll notice there are no page numbers! Instead, there are little check boxes you can tick, to remind yourself which pages you've read or 'done'.

I encourage you to have a notebook or a journal dedicated to your journey. You'll find space throughout the book to write, however, you might have additional reflections.

The book consists of five different elements. The following page shows you what these are, and serves as a legend for how to find them.

Half of the book is my thoughts and insights as they were when the book went to print.- they might have already changed by now. I decided to share them anyway because I learned that eliciting reflection in someone else is sometimes easier if they get stimulus from outside themselves.

This book doesn't contain explanations as to why I think what I think and how I got to any sort of conclusion because knowing that is irrelevant to your process. My thoughts result from the countless times I've had the pleasure of leading, facilitating, watching, hearing, reading, and coming to my understanding of so many encounters with other perspectives, situations, and behaviors.

You will agree, disagree, or feel indifferent ~~to~~ about what I write here. What matters most is that you take an honest and deep dive into an exploration of where your responses come from. I guarantee you will be surprised by what you find there.

The mirror-shard-marked pages are invitations to you. They are prompted reflections for you to play with. These are suggestions, and I encourage you to make them your own. However, explore your reactions, rejections, deviations, and the motivation to customize them.

Remember, the ending to this book is not defined and the invitation to reflect is a standing one. Many thoughts I share in here are things I never knew I even thought! Anything you will learn in the process will be an insight into 'a moment' And one day, those insights might change. This book serves as a reminder to revisit and reflect on these developments.

The following pages are a personal tribute to every person I've had the privilege to encounter.

This book is not about getting anything right or finished. It's about you and your mirror, and the reflections you find inside.

What you then share with the world is entirely your choice.

Enjoy.

Leonas

CONTENTS

Meditations

Insights

Notes to self

Stories

Your Reflections

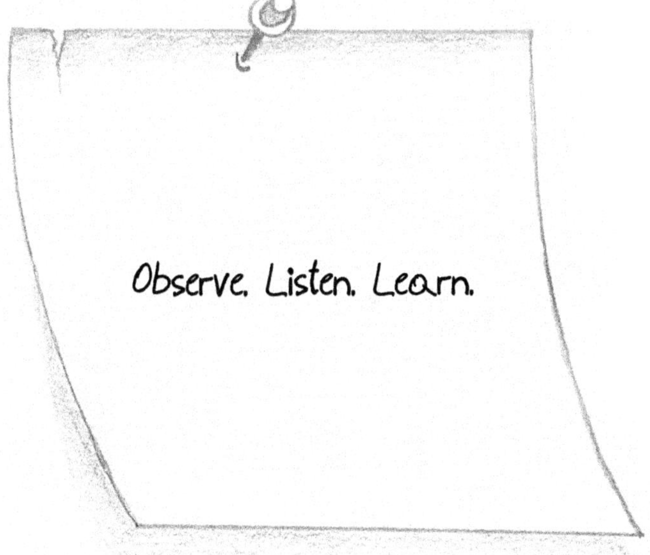
Observe. Listen. Learn.

A SAFE SPACE

BE HONEST WITH YOURSELF
ABOUT ALL YOUR REASONS FOR
WHY YOU DO YOUR JOB.
PIN THEM UP ON YOUR WALL
OF DESIRES

Dynamic Balance

All existence is about creating, keeping, restoring,
or presenting balance.

One side without the other loses its meaning.
Duality is two sides of the same thing.

Balance is not about extremes but about connection and dependency.
Balance can be adjusted and restored at any moment.
Balance is a static and a dynamic concept simultaneously.
Balance is crucial for impactful transformative experiences.

When we lack balance, we gravitate towards what we need.
Dis-balance leads to a sense of incompletion and lack of fulfillment.

Create sufficient countermeasure to avoid over-emphasis.
Consider when to create balance and when to let it emerge naturally.

The art is knowing when to create, guide and induce balance,
and when to let it emerge naturally.
There will never be perfect balance, but a dynamic sphere that needs
constant assessment and navigation.

Facilitation is balancing.

Dynamically.

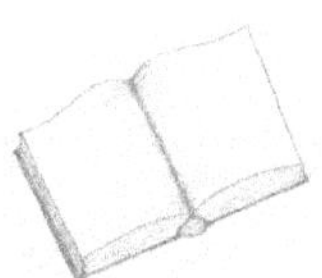

DRAW/WRITE/TELL A TALE FROM YOUR CHILDHOOD THAT IS ECHOED IN YOUR PRACTICE/WORK TODAY

Facilitation starts and ends with us.

Everything we do, think, and feel is rooted in our need to belong.

What we've discovered or read whenever we say we 'read the room' are assumptions.

Time is a common frame for a uniquely perceived concept.

We can call ourselves "a facilitator" in retrospect, but whether we ever facilitate another process is beyond our scope of influence.

The question "who is the most vulnerable?" will always be answered by our biases/counterbiases.

Co-facilitation can serve as a way of unconsciously projecting our shortcomings on our partner.

A "difficult" participant is someone who doesn't know what they need, nor how to communicate it to you.

IF YOU COULD CHOOSE JUST ONE ALTERNATIVE WORD FOR FACILITATION, IT WOULD BE

JUMP START

I look at my watch; my heart is pounding. Soon, the participants will arrive. Representatives of youth and women groups, I was told. I don't feel ready for my first-ever workshop. I wonder if one can ever be ready. Huh, it is too late now. I pause and look out into the auditorium. Like a theater, it has countless steps and many rows of seats covered in red fabric. It isn't the room that had been agreed upon, and the actual workshop space is reduced to the area between the stage and the first row. I will just make it work. My stomach's knots, the hot and cold shivers, and my restless pacing keep me busy. Meanwhile time is racing. I focus on setting up my carefully crafted materials. As a firm believer in visual learning, I am excited about the flipcharts as the main engagement tool for this experience. I detest technology in workshops.

"Hello?"

The first participant arrives, and my heart leaps. I crane my neck to see him, as the entrance door is hidden in the darkness far above me. He sounds older than I expected. I jog up the stairs and arrive a little breathless. "Welcome! Please, join me down here and find a seat." The last word sticks in my throat. The man is already seated. In his wheelchair.

"Is this it?" I hear the bright friendly voice of a second man. I spot his white cane enter the room before he does.

They had forgotten to tell me that a third group was invited – people with disabilities.

WRITE AND REHEARSE
A 3-MINUTE PITCH
(NO MORE, NO LESS) TELLING
ANYONE WHY THEY SHOULD BE
FACILITATED BY YOU

HOLDING SPACE

FORMULATE
YOUR 3 TOP LEARNINGS
IN THE ROLE OF FACILITATOR
AS SOUNDBITES

Underdiscussed Skills

The art of facilitation does not comprise a single skill. It is the application of a skillset. Unfortunately, some skills get more attention than others.

Confident Decision-Making
Analytical Observation
Saying No
Interrupting
Doing Nothing
Covert Deflection
Depersonification
Keeping Connection
Shuttle Facilitation
Environmental Awareness
Applied Empathy
Micro Decompression
Framing Metaphors
Mastering Inner Communication
Timely Patience
Participant Contribution Memory
Deduction
Remaining Unpredictable
Deciphering Uncrafted Feedback
Humble Curiosity
Sensitivity Intelligence
Appropriateness Consideration
Compartmentalization

BRAINDUMP ALL THE OVERRATED FACILITATION SKILLS YOU CAN THINK OF IN 10 MINUTES. TAKE AT LEAST A 30 MINUTE BREAK. WHEN YOU RETURN REFLECT ON WHY YOU THINK THEY ARE OVERRATED

Authority is not negative. Our use of it makes it so.

The real information can be found in why we find something to be irrational.

Neutrality is an unachievable, thus irrelevant concept.

If the participants are more observant of what happens in the room than us, we are not doing our job.

Our need to know everything that happens in the room is rooted in our desire to keep control.

The final determination of whether I was suitable for the group is always made by the participants in retrospect.

We are prone to imitating others, instead of becoming the model for others to imitate.

Trust is deeply paradoxical. It feeds off past experiences while being given in advance.

THINK OF YOUR TOP THREE
NON-NEGOTIABLES
AND DRAW AN IMAGE THAT
REPRESENTS
ALL OF THEM

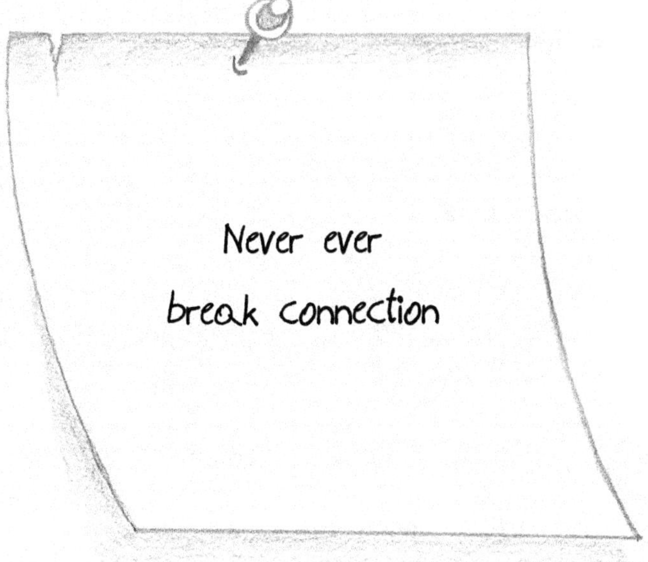
Never ever
break connection

ONLY HUMAN

My inner tension keeps rising. I am tired from not having slept much last night.

I watch them enter the room with their coffee mugs, smiling. They greet me and find their seats, getting ready for day two. Friendly, as if everything is okay and we will just carry over from the first day to the next.

Only, it is not the same. Yesterday at the same time, I was looking forward to working with them. This morning, I'd rather not be here.

I have no idea how this morning, hell, the first hour, is going to play out. The agenda my co-facilitator and I crafted so carefully has long been dismissed.

We start with small groups reflecting on the day before. I open up the floor and give them a chance to tell me, to my face, what they needed, wanted, and missed.

I wonder, will they tell me the things I have been hearing through other channels just last night and this morning?

I had become a scapegoat.

And here it comes.

They are harshly critical about how our process didn't meet their needs. They say it is our fault that they haven't talked about what they came here for. How we have wasted their time.

I look over to the leadership team, that just moments before signalled they had my back. To my astonishment they echo the message of their subordinates: one of fundamental disappointment in us and blame for not addressing important issues.

I am calm. I smile. Then comes the storm—even I don't see it coming.

It is like I am an onlooker.

"Let me step out of my facilitator role, for just a moment," I say. My smile, while still there, hardens.

I open my mouth to begin what I realize will be a longer speech.

"Thank you. I take every input on the process seriously and we will learn from this and adapt today accordingly.
Beyond that, however,

don't hold **me** responsible for **your** *bullshit*."

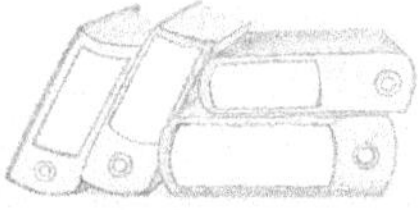

COLLECT ALL THE WAYS
YOU CAN IMAGINE SAYING "NO"
TO SOMEONE.
THEN RECORD YOURSELF
SAYING THEM

Some questions are not about getting an answer, but about remaining curious.

Whatever we do when leading a process will never be assessed by a group. It's done by each individual.

Our desperation to be perceived as authentic makes us become who we think the audience wants to see.

There is no one right way to facilitate. There are only right ways to facilitate.

Agendas, methods, courses, books are red herrings. Facilitation is actually all about winging it. And just all the time.

When we speak about "purpose" in facilitation we mostly refer to working purpose or intent.

The way to know a participant's deepest need/s is if we get them to push back. Until then, everyone works inside their comfort zones.

CRUSHED

What a fantastic week! The workshop and the conversations are mind-blowing. I am brimming with admiration for the people who shared insights into how they work daily to make the world a better place, fight injustice, and risk their lives. We planned this workshop with the utmost care and consent of all participants. We ran it outside their country of residence to ensure their safety. We even had to label the workshop something other than what we were discussing, and we crafted each piece of communication down to the last detail. All to protect everyone in attendance, and their work.

One particular participant stands out, who opens up about their work at a shadow organization. His organization is documenting atrocities being committed in his country, which would otherwise be forgotten. He is staunchly committed to creating a better future for his family in his homeland. He shares generously, and fearlessly provides incredible insights that are sure to stay with me long afterwards.

A week passes.

It's time for the debrief. I'm looking forward to hearing the feedback from the client, so I'm anything but prepared to hear news like this. "We had a leak," the lead facilitator starts. "Our friend who runs the shadow organization has officially been declared a traitor, with the death penalty waiting for him if he ever returns home."

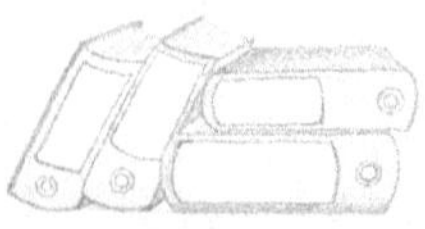

PICK ANY POINT IN TIME IN THE FUTURE
AND WRITE A LETTER FROM YOUR FUTURE SELF TO YOUR CURRENT SELF

The P-word

Power has many faces. It is visible and invisible. It is positive and negative. It is an enabler and a blocker. It creates change and destroys things.

Power is integral to human interaction. Even inclusive, democratic, fair, and equal groups build in power dynamics.

Power is found in and nourished by structural elements, like rules, agreements, and boundaries.

Power requires humility, responsibility, and respect. We must never forget that we are entrusted with this impactful gift.

Power allows us to connect with others and to ourselves. Power leads to self-determination and the ability to act as ourselves in an interaction.

Power presents an opportunity. It catalyzes transformation, enabling new ways, and guides people towards different perspectives.

Power is mandated. Being assigned gives us a formal acknowledgment of a role we must use with care. Sometimes self-mandating is required.

Power is perceived. When we enter a space, we are attributed power by everyone in it. This is informed by our posture, appearance, introduction, comparisons, or how we claim the space.

Power is a puzzle. It works best if we each hold a piece, instead of some grabbing many and others bearing none.

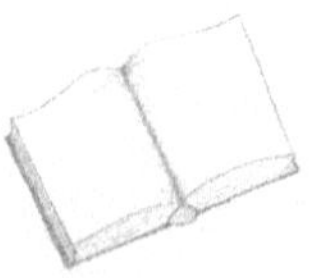

Facilitation builds on power dynamics. It starts with comprehending group dynamics, which is the essence of each process.

Facilitation is the execution of power. Stepping back is power. Stepping in is power. Stepping up is power.

Facilitators have power. It's part of the mandate. Distancing ourselves from power denies realities and limits our potential in any group. Distancing ourselves from power is misleading and deceiving. Distancing ourselves from power is evading responsibility.

Facilitators need power. Any sort of denial is based on our discomfort with being attributed power externally. Any dislike of power is rooted in our experiences.

Facilitators want power. We want to stand in front of the groups, do impactful work, and be acknowledged for that.

Facilitators without power are lame ducks.

If we don't claim our power, someone else will.

It is a facilitator's duty to really understand themselves.

While it is crucial to try to listen for what is not being said, what we don't hear remains an assumption until it's shared.

Every design will mirror the preferences of the one facilitating.

Questions are a tool disguised as a normal communication pattern.

Trust is the highest level of vulnerability.

The role of a facilitator is not to make the people in attendance fit the purpose

Since the future cannot be predicted, every single thing a facilitator does carries risk.

Frameworks are wonderful structures to hide behind.

TAKE 10 MINUTES TO FILL YOUR INTERRUPTION TOOLBOX

Every single encounter
can be meaningful

WRITE A SHORT PROFILE
(MAX 200 WORDS) ABOUT
WHAT YOU WOULD DO
PROFESSIONALLY, IF YOU WERE
BANNED FROM FACILITATING
(IN ANY ROLE)

DEMONS

Out of the box thinking is not out of the box doing.

Holding a space is the job of everyone present. Claiming that one person can (or must) do that is not just pretentious, it's wild.

Reading the room is not enough if we don't know what to do with what we read.

Engagement is more "subjective assessment" and less "reliable indicator".

When you say someone is irrational you're saying your perspective is the universal baseline for rationality.

Our ambition level is both friend and foe. The art is to know which one to invite, when.

Protecting and promoting individuality when practicing facilitation is a non-negotiable.

MAP WHAT CONNECTION MEANS TO YOU

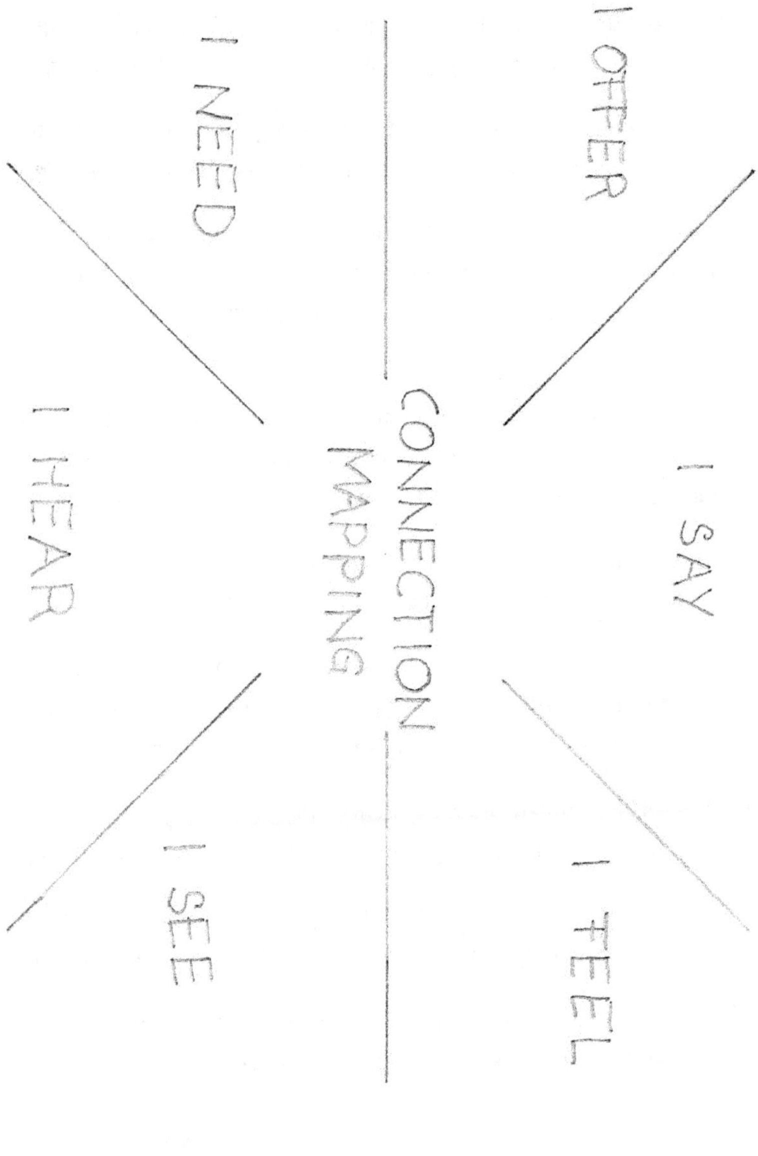

I SAY
I OFFER
I FEEL
CONNECTION
MAPPING
I NEED
I SEE
I HEAR

Discoveries

Pizza baker. The world's best pizzas are made with no more than five basic ingredients. The same goes for workshops.

Receptionist. You have seconds to connect with people personally. Human connection is the highest priority.

Hairdresser. Follow the participants along their journey and learn about them while you continuously do your magic.

Outdoor guide. Be familiar with the territory you are taking people into. Or have the awareness and skills to guide them through unfamiliar territory.

Rugby referee. Be clear and concise in your communication. Too many words confuse the audience and are open to interpretation.

Construction worker. There is always a way to work with what you have. Sometimes you need to demolish it to repair it. Other times a quick patch-up is what's needed to work on it in the long term.

Actor. Hardly anything follows a script. Sometimes you need to improvise, sometimes you need to apologize, sometimes you need to reset. Every alternative is a good one.

Magician. We are easily distracted by a reality that we create in our minds. Use this effect to help participants see what they don't.

Diver. No step is taken without a brief. Be clear in giving instructions and reassure yourself that everyone has understood.

Sports psychologist. Most of the workshop happens in everyone's head. It is important to work, use mental tools, and constantly connect the cognitive with the physical.

Profiler. Everything that happens in a workshop gives us information about the participants, their behavior, their mental models and their relationship to others.

Clown. Only you know your idea. Act in every situation as if it was intended. And, have complete faith in your next act.

Flight attendant. A constant balance between individuals' needs and responsibility for the collective, (and the nerves to stay calm in the face of turbulence!) are essential to keep in mind when facilitating.

Captain. Sometimes hard decisions must be made, and it can be a lonely job. However, not taking them or dodging the responsibility is not in the interest of passengers.

Firefighter. No problem will be solved if we do not dare go to the core of its existence.

Teacher. Build a toolbox that allows varied ways of instructing. This creates attention, interest, motivation and engagement.

Stand-up comedian. It's all about creating the first moment where the audience relaxes their shoulders.

Tennis player. No matter how badly a workshop is going, there is always a recovery. Just adapt the tactics.

Airport security. Always ask for permission when intervening with someone's autonomy.

Too many words dilute information, give direction,
and rob participants of their own learning experience.

The term "group" is a simplification and generalization
of highly complex, unique, dynamic systems.

Facilitation isn't a profession that needs certification.
The ultimate accreditation is being trusted to facilitate
a process by participants.

Everything we do reveals what we care about, what we
fear, and what doesn't concern us.

No closing statement will ever be good enough to
capture the essence of an experience, which is why
every closing statement is perfect and captures the
experience.

We can never empower. We only can help create spaces
where people dare, and learn, to empower themselves.

We use words for reductive purposes, hoping to portray
a shared worldview. We would be better off using words
to explore different worldviews.

Sometimes going slow will get you there faster.
Sometimes going faster will make it easier to learn.

WRITE 5 THINGS THAT MAKE YOU INDISPENSIBLE

Coherent Presence

Please select from the following, Mr Thomas Lahnthaler.

Multiple choice (More than one answer permitted.)

a) Be authentic.
b) Be yourself.
c) Adapt to the context.
d) Be fully present.
e) All of the above.
f) None of the above.

Answer

e) and f).
Authenticity depends on the audience.
Being yourself can jar with the context.
Adapting to the context is fakery.
The choices a) b) c) and d) presume that presence is static,
while it is a range.

Being true to ourselves means we know
where we are, where we end, and where others begin.

Compromise is possible beyond that boundary of self.

Being true to the situation is the act of understanding and
respecting the boundaries that arise in any given context.

Being true to others' perceptions is not giving up yourself.
It is the art of being yourself while meeting them in their reality.

Coherent presence is the intersection
of these three boundaried worlds.

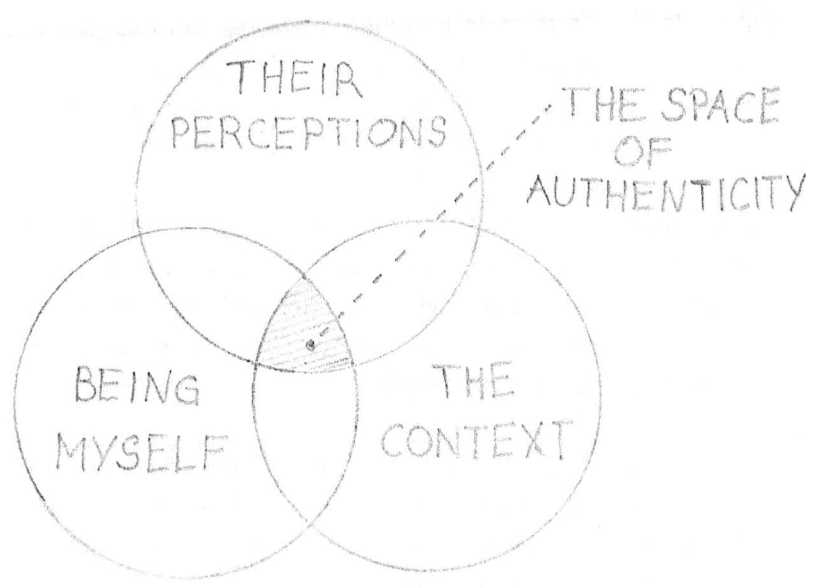
THEIR PERCEPTIONS
THE SPACE OF AUTHENTICITY
BEING MYSELF
THE CONTEXT

FEEDBACK

The management team from my NGO client calls me for a meeting to discuss my perspective on how the workshop went. We go through the session and the topics we covered. It is all to their satisfaction. They are particularly thrilled about the engagement of the non-management staff-base. Interestingly, most staff in those departments are nationals from this country, while only one member of the management team is a local. Historically management had been critical of local staff members for holding back and for not participating as much as they should have.

I know the exact reasons why. I saw it play out in the workshop. In other words once you see it, you cannot unsee discriminatory, racist behavior. The head of the team and I have worked together many times. She is a fan of my work and has even become a close friend.

I listen to them for a bit longer, sharing perspectives, before they turn to me. "Thomas, what do you think? How did it go?" I pause for a second, look at them evenly, and take a steadying breath before I speak.

Every group is uniquely diverse.

The idea that there is too little work for too many facilitators is a defiance of simple math.

We can be our most authentic selves; whether the world perceives this is entirely out of our hands.

There are no good or bad facilitators. There are facilitators whose approach we like and those whose we do not.

Often the most insights can be found in a failed intention.

Filling the facilitator space and role requires the act of demanding authority.

When you focus too much on a process's purpose, you influence the process itself.

Without striving for active resistance from participants you won't design the most memorable experience.

TAKE YOUR FAVORITE METHOD, TOOL, FRAMEWORK AND THINK ABOUT WHAT MAKES IT YOUR FAVORITE. TAKE IT APART; THEN REASSEMBLE IT AS A COMPLETELY NEW ONE FOR A COMPLETELY DIFFERENT PURPOSE

Accepting an assignment to lead others without "knowing yourself"—really well—is negligent.

Being liked is not a necessity and can be a nuisance for effective facilitation.

Every decision, activity, and action we lead as facilitators is based on the assumption that it benefits the group. But we only ever discover the benefits when all is said and done.

Co-creation is not the same as co-decision-making.

Everything is driven by our need to belong.

Whoever shows up is the right participant.

Regardless of effort and awareness, our interpretation of the dynamics in the group will always be biased.

Until you connect with the group you can't call yourself a facilitator.

Life is not a framework. Using frameworks to navigate human dynamics is ironic, limiting and paradoxical.

The problem with listening to those who speak up first is that it's convenient to believe they speak for the group. Especially when this happens to speak to our own needs.

Harmony without friction is avoidance. (There is nothing satisfying or exciting about hearing everything in C major).

Facilitation is a unique combination of skills, every single time. This combination cannot be taught in a course or book.

Everyone present reads the room at any given time. We're just not all referring to the same manual.

You will never be able to connect with the group if you cannot connect with yourself.

Post-workshop come-down is real and inevitable. Our task is to ready the participants and ourselves for it.

DRAW A ROADMAP OF THE EMOTIONAL JOURNEY OF THE LAST GROUP PROCESS YOU FACILITATED.
PLEASE COUNT YOURSELF AS PART OF THE GROUP

YOUR SAFETY PROTOCOL.
(JOT DOWN EVERYTHING
YOU NEED TO FEEL SAFE)

REALITIES MEET

It's a rare quiet moment in my house. I'm sitting on the sofa and pick up a book. I am a few pages in when I hear my three-year-old girl approach. I don't look up but notice she's standing there, watching me.

After a while, she asks curiously: "What are you doing?"
I look up. "I'm reading."

Unimpressed, she replies: "No, you are not."

Now, she has got my attention: "What do you think I am doing?"

My little girl pauses, looking up to search for a thought. She studies my face for clues: "I don't know, but you are not reading."

I try to hide my smile and acknowledge her predicament: "What makes you think that?"

She rolls her eyes at my stupidity: "You are not saying anything." She turns and walks away.

I sit with this moment for a while, playing it through, wondering who taught whom at that moment?

COLLECT A LIST OF ADDITIONAL PROMPTS FOR FUTURE REFLECTION. RETURN AT A LATER STAGE TO DIVE INTO THEM

Saying "I don't know what to do next" doesn't make you a bad facilitator. It makes you a relatable human being.

Facilitation mostly is a trade-off between acting in our perception of the needs of the group or being our most authentic selves.

Facilitation depends on the awareness, acceptance, and comfort one has with one's own authority.

Working purposes are dangerous concepts. They point to a direction, thereby fooling everyone—including us—into believing that this is the only and final destination.

Emotions are like trains. They often come with a delay.

Facilitators must always strive to adjust the process, for everyone to feel they are in the right place.

Co-facilitation is not more challenging than facilitating alone. It only feels that way because our partner reveals denied truths about ourselves.

DRAW A GARDEN THAT GROWS THE SOURCES OF YOUR REGENERATION

How we formulate instructions is the result of our own needs.

The most freeing way to manage your own expectations is not to have any.

There is a gross mismatch between input, design, or other form of directing the process—and the idea of neutrality.

Getting bored while facilitating means we have disconnected from the group and its dynamics.

The title of facilitator doesn't automatically mean you have this role and responsibility. This mandate is bestowed on you by the participants. What you can do is be willing to step forward and accept it.

Using frameworks is an illusory attempt to make the unknown more predictable by creating an invisible cage and clipping wings.

Even the best process doesn't help poor content.

THINK ABOUT A FUNDAMENTAL BELIEF THAT YOU HOLD ABOUT WORKING WITH GROUPS AND ANSWER THE FOLLOWING EXPLORATIONS:

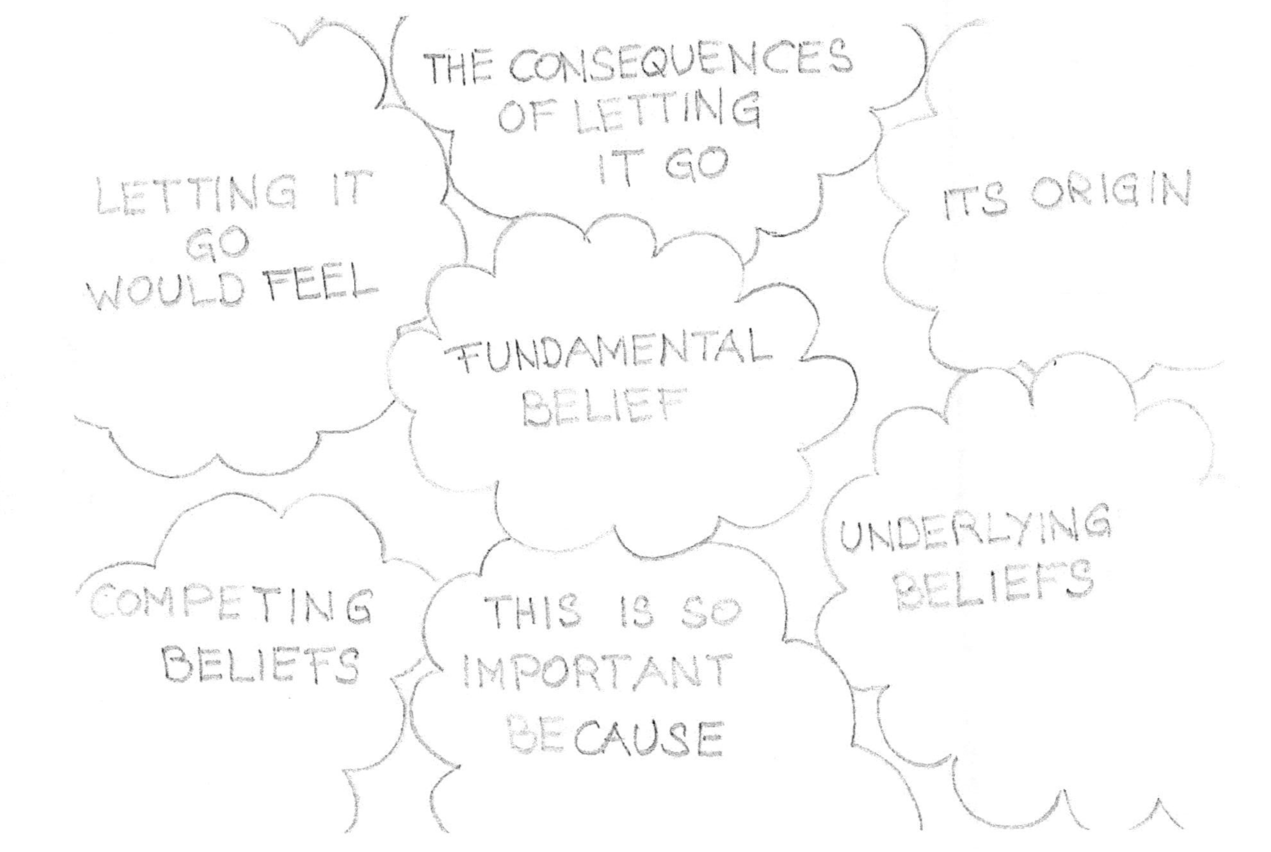
THE CONSEQUENCES OF LETTING IT GO
ITS ORIGIN
LETTING IT GO WOULD FEEL
FUNDAMENTAL BELIEF
UNDERLYING BELIEFS
COMPETING BELIEFS
THIS IS SO IMPORTANT BECAUSE

PROJECTION

FIND A SAFEWORD
TO GET YOU OUT OF
FACILITATION MODE

LOSING COUNT

Finally, all the participants have arrived—an amazingly diverse group of all ages and demographics. I am to guide them through a systemic conflict analysis of their country. A country that has a violent history which, in recent years, has brutally resurfaced. Given the seminar's sensitivity, and how tense the local situation is, we run the sessions in a neighboring country to ensure the participants' safety.

I am ready and confident. I know the methodology thoroughly because I have run the workshop many times before. The energy and curiosity in the room are contagious. As always, I begin interactively. I encourage collective experiences for group cohesion.

"I just need to split you up into five random groups" I tell them. I start counting out loud, gesturing respectfully with an open palm toward each person so they know which group they've been assigned to. "One, two, three, four, five, one, two, three."

"Mr Thomas," a young man gently interrupts me. I wonder if I will ever get used to being called that. "Can I share something with you?"

"Absolutely. Just remember your numbers, please, if I've given you one. They can be easy to forget," I call to the audience lightly, though I receive no smiles in return.

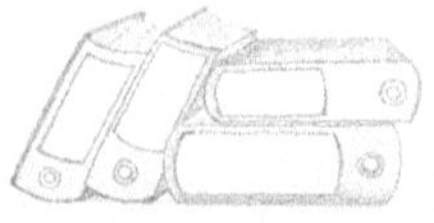

The young man continues: "We don't count people in our country."

"Oh?" I am genuinely surprised.

"Yes, it reminds us of when the militias came to our villages. They counted us out to work out who to kill."

Craft emergence

SKETCH ON A LOOSE PAGE WHAT
IS HOLDING YOU BACK FROM
BEING THE BEST VERSION YOU
CAN BE. READ IT OUT LOUD.
DESTROY THE PAGE

Gifted Feedback

The thoughtful
This is something special, given with great consideration of the
recipient's wishes. It demonstrates an appreciation for who they are
and how they show up in the giver's life.

The intentional
Gifts are frequently used to create impact on the other person
and achieve something. Whether this is courting, apologizing,
or simply seeking affection, it comes with a clear intention.

The selfish
Presents are sometimes anchored in the need and desire to give
something, irrespective of the other person needing it.

The symbolic
Some things are gifted have little practical use; however, they
represent values, emotions, or memories of the relationship.

The helpful
Some gifts obviously focus on trying to help the recipient with a
problem or a challenge that they are facing.

The pragmatic
The gifts that we neither want nor use with joy, and still convince
us that they are ideal.

The self-desired
Ironically, some gifts are given because the givers desire them
themselves.

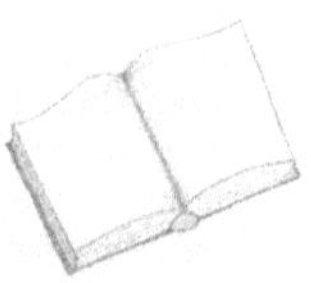

The general item
Some gifts are actually not only for the recipient but can be used by other people around.

The subtle message
Some gifts carry subtle messages both positive or negative that the sender might not be able, willing, or daring to convey directly.

The useless
Then there are those gifts that no matter which way you turn them, they have little use, message or meaning.

The recycled
Sometimes gifts are reused, or things we received that we couldn't use, and pass on for the next person to use.

The mood-lifter
Sometimes a gift is intended to make the person (and everyone around) laugh and happy, and help them forget about worries, problems, and negative emotions.

The controller
Then there are gifts that are given with the aim to change the recipient. They interfere with their autonomy.

The spontaneous
There was no prior intention of giving a gift but suddenly it felt like the right thing to do. They usually come from a good place.

Feedback is not a gift. It is a reality check.

CLOSE YOUR EYES AND IMAGINE A SCENARIO THAT MAKES YOU (UN)COMFORTABLE AND (IN)SECURE. TRY TO IDENTIFY WHAT IT IS THAT TRIGGERS THESE FEELINGS IN YOU AND HOW YOU USUALLY RESPOND

What seems opposite is interconnected. The one gives the other meaning and relevance. So, inclusion is dependent on exclusion for it to have meaning.

Facilitators cannot hold other facilitators accountable for their facilitation; only participants can.

Continuously assess your connection with the group.

Is this is your responsibility? The answer must be an unconditional yes.

Not all disruptions are disruptive. When they are, prioritize them.

Creative thinking doesn't depend on psychological safety; sharing what we have discovered does.

The professional in us will try to stay impartial; the human in us will lean towards the people we most relate to, or who support our approach and ideas.

Regardless of the group's makeup, our authority will always be tested by someone somehow.

Facilitation demands the ability to continuously make a mental shift of attendance, without ever switching off entirely.

We don't learn facilitation; we learn individual skills that we then turn into our approach when we facilitate.

Getting extroverts to reflect in silence is just as hard as getting introverts to share.

Even if facilitators are not parents, there is a correlation between these two roles, skillsets, and the power of modelling for those who are always watching.

Triggering someone negatively is ridiculously easy. Reversing this is one of the hardest things to do.

Every group experience leaves an emotional footprint.

Self-awareness is a lifelong process.

Every facilitation is the first time.

IDENTIFY YOUR CORE VALUES.
THEN RANK YOUR TOP 3

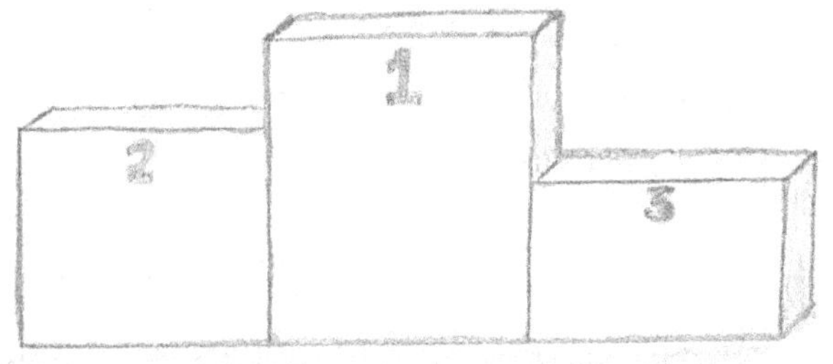

Humble Curiosity

Curiosity

...is an innate infinite resource.

...turns into a skill with practice.

...has more faces than questions.

...must be about continuous discoveries, not final answers.

...must be expressed considerately.

...is guided by humility instead of inquisition and overreach.

...requires you sharing your own perspectives.

...depends on perspectives and views not being superior.

...has the aim of discovering others' realities to expand your own.

...encourages you to discover to how anything relates to you.

...of the humblest type is all about discovering yourself.

My limit is not their limit

WRITE A SHORT STORY OF YOUR FONDEST MEMORY IN AN ORGANISED GROUP SETTING – BE SURE TO GO AND TELL IT TO SOMEONE

Transferring feedback from one workshop to another is of limited value.

Being unconventional requires knowing the conventions first.

It doesn't make us less authentic if another person thinks we are inauthentic.

The uniqueness of every facilitation, every participant, every experience must always be respected.

Agendas give the illusion of familiar territory; meanwhile, we enter a world of the unknown with every single process.

It is not your job to satisfy others or be a scapegoat.

Focusing only on achieving the pre-defined purpose creates tunnel vision, and blinds everyone to opportunities.

Comfort zones aren't called that because they are comfortable, but because they are more familiar than whatever we anticipate lies beyond them.

NOTE DOWN
HOW YOU DETERMINE
WHO IS THE MOST VULNERABLE
IN THE GROUP AND WHERE YOU
LEARNT TO DO IT THAT WAY

Too little time means
too high ambitions

FIND THE SONG THAT SUMS YOU UP AND HAVE A KARAOKE SESSION IN FRONT OF YOUR MIRROR

Facilitator Blues

4|4 𝄋

Workshop ||:Noise Silence Commotion Stillness | Energy
Emptiness Answers Contemplations |

Pride Sadness Doubt Laughter | Exclusion Connection Loneliness
Experience |

Confidence Vulnerability Answers Questions | Ecstasy Exhaustion
Direction Disorientation |

Joy Grief Knowing Wondering | Enjoying Longing Surprise
Anticipation |

Belonging Abandonment Success Failure | Presence Distraction
Endurance Relief | Acceptance Reframing Closure Moving on :||

Going through the motions | Different notes | Same tune ||

WRITE DOWN 10 FUTURE COMMITMENTS FOR YOUR OWN PRACTICE

Commitments
Commitments

THE PREROGATIVE

The two men are staring at their phones. The air fills with rising tension. I can't connect with anyone. The third member, and the only woman in the group, makes a half-hearted attempt to help me out by answering my questions and appearing engaged. The men don't even hide their disinterest and mostly ignore me, my prompts, and my input. They leave the room about every 10 minutes to take a call. The content is relevant for their roles, no doubt, but nothing about this workshop sits right.

They are on edge, tense, and extremely stressed; I see it, hear it, and sense it. When they return from the break I have designated, I make one last attempt. I ask them to give me five minutes of their attention and after that they'll be free to go if they choose so, with no repercussions with management. They shrug in agreement.

I mirror the behavior I have observed since we started, in detail. The look on their faces is of disbelief. Now, I have their attention.

I ask them what they would do if they were in my place.

I don't get an answer, exactly. One of the men say, "I am just not sure why I am here. The workshop is pretty interesting, but we literally just had training on something very similar. And to be honest, work is killing me." The others nod intensely.

I respond: "I understood that you wanted this training and asked for this workshop in particular." They all burst out laughing. "No, we asked for support to help us not to burn out." My confusion is difficult to camouflage.

"The purpose of this session, I was told by your management, was to build your crisis leadership skills further." The man who has hardly said anything and has been buried in his phone most during the session, glances up. "That's their purpose, and yours. Not ours."

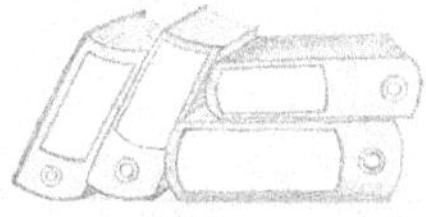

Never steal
anyone's thunder

PICK YOUR RELATIONSHIP TO RISK AND CERTAINTY.

Crash-Test-Dummie

Adrenaline Junkie

Doomsday Prepper

Mr./Mrs. Play-it-safe

To "read the room" is a subjective skillset that cannot
be taught.

We identify the most vulnerable in a group based on
our projections or assumptions.

Facilitators sharing knowledge with only facilitators
will lead to stagnation and irrelevance of the profession.

Professional facilitators make it our job to help people
avoid verbal shortcuts, while we continue to use
jargon and empty simplifications around our work
of facilitation.

Representing facilitated sessions as "fun" creates
a misleading, misrepresentative and misconceptualised
picture, and damages the potential of effective
and impactful facilitation.

Understanding every group's unique communication
pattern is the key to connected facilitation.

Everyone is a facilitator at some point in their lives.

Sometimes you have to use precisely what you
desperately want to change to achieve that change.

MAKE A HOW-TO GUIDE THAT OUTLINES EXACTLY WHAT YOU DO WHEN YOU READ THE ROOM

DEFLATION

The small group, whose process I'm facilitating, has reached its limits. What is supposed to be a team development session on strategic planning has soured over two days. Underlying frictions emerge. I stop the process and suggest a conflict moderation instead. I get the go-ahead.

The next day we start. It is honest, deep, and emotionally demanding because of a peculiar tension: between high personal regard for each other, deep friendship, and significant professional differences. The one who struggles most with this paradox is the team leader. He is also the one at whom most of the issues are directed.

We work through each one. The team members are relieved, though exhausted. Workshop done.

During my debrief call the following day, the team leader expresses his appreciation for how I handled the situation; how satisfied he is with the laying of certain issues on the table that have been brewing under the surface. He plans to develop some ideas further and wants my opinion on them. We agree to have a call the following week.

I do receive a call from him the next week, earlier than expected.

He sounds flat. "Hi, Thomas. I wanted to thank you again for your support to our team. It was invaluable and I have given a lot of thought to what happened during the process you facilitated.

I've resigned."

WRITE A POEM ABOUT YOUR RELATIONSHIP TO RESISTANCE

Belonging

What if we …
stopped cutting realities adrift, over and over again?
embraced our desire to be part of a group, instead of fighting it?
declined to dance with eternal boundary crossing?
acknowledged this inner battle as fundamentally counter-intuitive?
understood that holding space has the prerequisite that everyone
belongs?
recognized that belonging comes before safety?

What if it …
takes humans to make humans feel they belong?
takes belonging for us to be human?

What if people …
permitted themselves to belong?
stopped so cautiously guarding space?
resisted repeated invitations to fend for themselves,
or on behalf of others?

What if such …
self-protection, though noble, causes disconnect?
noble disconnection was self-harming?

What if this …
leads to us not being the best we can?

What if it were …
recognized that belonging is a key criterion for any leader-
facilitator. For anyone?
allowed for the orator-leader to accept they belong, rather than
keep lingering on the outskirts?

What if all we do is …
surrender to our basic need?
become aware of denial?
open an unattended door to belonging, in that space we so
desperately fight to belong?

What if …
all we do …

is belong?

What if?

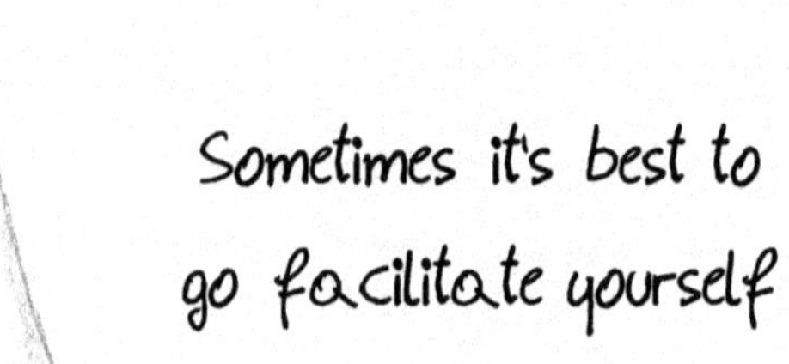
Sometimes it's best to
go facilitate yourself

DRAW THE IMAGE THAT COMES TO MIND WHEN YOU THINK OF YOUR FACILITATION

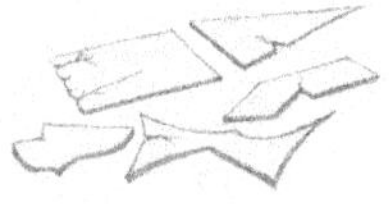

READING THE ROOM

Any information about the group before we actually meet as a group must be considered hearsay.

The vast majority of what we do will be unrecognized and forgotten.

Our favorite framework is a dead giveaway of our biases and preferences.

The phenomenon of the certified facilitator creates the illusion that such a person is equipped to facilitate any situation. They are not.

Telling them "what" is essential; telling them "how" is stealing their learning experience.

You are a hypocrite if you take responsibility for a process's failure and you deny having contributed to a process's success.

Emotional detachment during a session does not protect anyone from the feelings that follow.

Facilitators have no right to criticize other facilitators unless they have been a participant in that process.

Presence is participation

COVERT ASSUMPTIONS

This is going well. Maybe a bit slower than expected. Still, I feel we are on track. I enjoy eavesdropping on the conversations and listening to the intense exchanges. It is a fascinating group, with the majority being young Afghan men and women, mixed with some international staff. It is exciting to work with them on one of my favorite topics—alternative conflict resolution.

The initial reservation and shyness has faded. I was worried that only the international staff would be vocal and might overshadow the Afghan participants' experiences and perspectives by taking up too much space. None of that is happening. The tone is cheerful and friendly, and despite the seriousness and relevance of the topic, the mood seems light. I've spent time getting to know them personally, like listening to these early twenty-somethings share proud parenting moments. I was also open about myself and how I ended up there. It's crucial, as our backgrounds are so different.

I am about to transition into the topics of the day after a short check-in, when a young Afghan man raises his hand and starts talking with a genuine expression of concern. "Mr. Thomas. I have talked with the others; about what you told us about your life. And we all agree. You must really hate women and children."

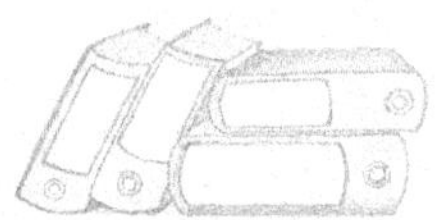

WRITE YOUR PERSONAL REMINDER OF YOUR MOTIVATION TO HELP PEOPLE. BE REALLY HONEST. THIS IS FOR YOUR EYES ONLY, UNLESS YOU DECIDE TO SHARE IT

Prison

Rules are intended to keep everyone safe. That goes for prisons and workshops alike. Safe from what or whom? The others (inmates, participants)? From us (facilitators, or prison guards), or themselves (the inmates as individuals)? If we need a set of rules in place then we are already prejudiced. It assumes that a scenario is sure to arise that requires them. Setting up rules without knowing of any actual danger, threat or crime is akin to a preemptive sentencing. Anyone present becomes guilty of potentially doing something to harm the group. *What does that make us, the judge? Who gave us that mandate?*

IIIIIIIIIIIIIIIIIIIIIIIIIIIIIIIIIIIIIIIIIIIIIIIIIIIIIIIIIIIIIIIIIIIIIIII

Psychological safety for everyone? In prisons, while the guards and the rest of the population are kept safe from everyone 'on the inside', the safety between the inmates is arguably the least guarded boundary of all. We are endangered when we rely on the rules as a protective element. Because compliance, respect— obedience—are still required for such rules to be effective. Rules 'guard the space' and aim to regulate interaction. But 'on the inside' there is little or nothing to leverage, to enforce them. Other than violence and punishment. Do we, and should we operate in such a punitive manner 'on the outside'? *What does that make us, referee? Who gave us that mandate?*

Waking sleeping dogs. (Or why rules only make rulebreakers smile). Let's say we set artificial boundaries to level the playing field, to protect the less secure from the powerful. But we soon forget that it's an illusion, and it quickly becomes our reality. Everyone will try to test how much leeway there really is. That means by-passing, tweaking, and pushing how far we can go before we are called out. This creates a resistance that teaches the wily ones to manipulate the ground rules and escape punishment. Rules are a fantasy invented by those who think they have the right to make them in the first place. *What does that make us, the instigator? Who gave us that mandate?*

||||||||||||||||||||||||||||||||||||||||||||||||||||||||||||||

Who makes the rules anyway? What if we left it to the inmates (if it's not the wardens or guards)!? Imagine we set the task for inmates to create a set of agreements? If we did, wouldn't the 'alpha types' decide on what those should look like? This would sully the playing field and set an imbalance from the outset.
Or would we open the doors to manipulators, where debts and allegiances could form before we even started? And how could we ever find a way that everyone really agrees? Would we leave it to the inmates to sort out different opinions or regulate? Without any rules from an external entity? *What does that make us, the game master? Who gave us that mandate?*

Simple guiding principles could be presented as an alternative to rules for the prison system. When the inmates are given ideas and aims for experiments, they might ignore how principles are interpreted. They might not embrace the guidelines at all. Certain elements are concrete: a space to discuss and exchange views on the interpretation with no rules or principles in place yet. Alternatively, an external authority defines them for the inmates. That leads us straight back to the authoritarian concept. Oh and yes—what if we ignore guiding principles entirely, in the process? *What does that make us, the know-it-all? Who gave us that mandate?*

||||||||||||||||||||||||||||||||||||||||||||||||||||||||||||||||||||||||

What sort of environment do rules create? Rules create a space where our learning and development is driven by essential external interactions and the main goal is to survive. Rules suggest that without them the climate could be unpredictable (read: unsafe) or dangerous. The rules define how far you can explore. And yet we know the boundaries are artificial. We cannot expect to create a space for emergence if we set boundaries on how far this emergence can go. *What does that make us, the dictator? Who gave us that mandate?*

Rules create different worlds. Rules are an artificial set of boundaries that create a divide. Those who follow them and those who don't … on the inside and the outside. This attitude doesn't mirror the outside world. When inmates re-enter the real world, they must adjust to the 'real' context. They could try to transfer them 'from the inside to the outside', but there are different rules when you are free. If the 'inside' rules worked in their favor they want to keep them. But who is to say they will find such rules to observe 'on the outside'? If reforming convicts, now in the community, continue to operate by the rules from 'the inside' they will be judged for it. *What does that make us, the social experimenter? Who gave us that mandate?*

||||||||||||||||||||||||||||||||||||||||||||||||||||||||||||||||||||||||||

Aren't we really the ones who want rules most? How safe would participants (inmates) feel if the 'protectors' aren't feeling safe? From a prison guard's view, would they be able to guard without such rules? Is this maybe the truth behind wanting rules? How do we feel about operating in a lawless environment? Maybe it would require us to dive deep, and meet participants as individuals in a set of unpredictable reactions and dynamics. Aren't we insistent about regulating a space while hiding behind the premise of safety for everyone? *What does that make us, the undercover agent? Who gave us that mandate?*

Only you know your intent

FILL IN THIS COLLECTOR'S CARD WITH WHAT YOU WOULD DO IF COULD MAGICALLY REINVENT YOURSELF

Facilitation is an ancient concept whose soul gets crushed by modern interpretations.

Every detail and piece of information we receive before a session makes us more prone to confirmation bias.

Authenticity is not the same as transparency. We aren't less authentic because we're not being transparent.

Not everything needs to be reflected.

Without sense-making, 'reading the room' is an empty application of our senses.

Designing an agenda is making a map of our assumptions.

Sufficient instructions can end with: "the instructions are complete and thought through."

No framework is universal.

THESE ARE MY TRAUMA(S) I AM TRYING TO SOLVE THROUGH MY PRACTICE

Hit them with their quotes

ENERGY MATCHING

We are pumped. This must be one of the best designs my partner and I have ever come up with. This is not going to be 'just another team development' workshop. We have twists, provocations, problems to explore, all tied together by the theme of elevating this team to version 2.0.

The participants all take their seats and ooze self-confidence. They have been the most successful team in their company for years. Their performance is so high that the three teams after them, combined, can't match them.

The session starts well and everyone enjoys it. Maybe a bit too much. With every challenge they master, their arrogance detracts from a focus on their learning.

Clearly, they function well as a team. Maybe a bit too well. My partner and I now understand the team leader's real problem. This self-assurance obscures team members' blind spots: they are stagnating, subtly but steadily losing motivation.

"Is this all you got?" one of them grins.

I glance across to my partner. With a synchronized nod we agree to deploy our never-been-used back-up: an untested, controversial and potentially inflammatory approach to team development.

Let's crush them.

WRITE A LETTER TO THE PERSON WHO IS YOUR GREATEST INSPIRATION AS A FACILITATOR, THANKING THEM AND EXPLAINING WHAT YOU ADMIRE ABOUT THEM, AND HOW YOU WANT TO BE DIFFERENT FROM THEM. THEN SEND IT, BURN IT OR DESTROY IT

Neutrality is a name for the myth that our presence, words, and actions could ever have no influence on perception, people, context or result.

Wherever people are, some form of facilitation is present.

Claiming responsibility for the process is not owning the process.

There are neither good nor bad frameworks.

Explanations are distractions from the essential message.

Our assessment of someone being vulnerable will influence how we interact with them.

Every small change in the environment has an (occasionally severe) impact on the group.

Expectations are obstacles to connection.

THE OPPOSITE OF FACILITATION
IN ONE WORD ONLY

Make them
forget their expectations

Change is simultaneously a constant, a process, a means, a by-product, and an outcome. We make our lives difficult by forgetting this continuity.

Ignoring and denying the emotional aftermath of everyone in a group process dehumanizes the profession of facilitation, the process of facilitation and all the people involved in a facilitated experience.

I am slow to judge another facilitator. Because if I do, I am making a patronizing assumption that I would have done "something better".

"To be authentic" is empty advice that lacks substance, instruction, and universal understanding.

The fewer answers we give, the more they will remember the session.

Facilitation doesn't always require a problem.
To be able to expand someone's comfort zone we first require awareness about their boundaries.

Trust is strongest and most vulnerable if it is unconditional. For it to be unconditional we must let go of expectations.

TAKE A WALK AND REFLECT ON "WHO IS LEFT?" IF YOU WERE STRIPPED OF ALL YOUR FRAMEWORKS AND TOOLS

WHO IS ACTUALLY "THE GROUP"?

Humans
before participants

WRITE THE QUOTE THAT EVERYONE SHOULD REMEMBER YOU FOR

Everything you do as a facilitator carries risk. There are no safe choices.

Frameworks are elegantly camouflaged boxes to unify impossibly diverse experiences.

Facilitators are there to assist, help, support, guide, advise, push, encourage, provoke, navigate. Never to serve.

A safe space means that what happens in the facilitation space stays in the facilitation space.

If you are entrusted to facilitate you are also entrusted with authority.

Beware that every experience creates a tribal language unknown to non-participants.

Nobody owns the process—everybody does.

Questions always induce a power dynamic.

GROUP NEEDS

NUT OF WAR

It's time to return to the session after a morning tea break. The participants come from two different countries, and we have everyone working on parallel tracks to analyze conflict contexts. This is a highly sensitive process and my co-facilitator and I have each been guiding one group through the intense, deep and demanding conversations.

Before we recommence, one group mills about one of their members—a young woman in panic. She cannot get enough air!

Once the ambulance arrives and the paramedics have attended to the patient, they rush her away. Shock and concern remain in the participants' faces, including the group that has not yet worked with her closely.

Everyone is shaken but they agree to continue to working in plenary, while we wait for news.

We are all thankful to get word that the young woman is stable after suffering an acute allergic reaction. At the hospital they found out, that in addition to a known peanut allergy she was vigilant about, she has a macadamia nut allergy.

The other group had brought a delicacy as a gift to share at morning tea. It contained these culprit nuts. Like everyone, the young woman had eaten some during the break. With this explanation, both groups seem relieved and prepare to continue the process.

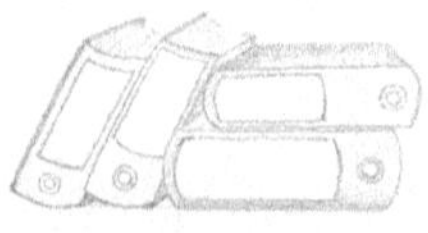

Just as my co-facilitator takes his group to their breakout room, one the elders in my group takes the word.

"What are we going to do about them?", he says to his peers, his eyes fixed on the other group.

Then he stands up, screaming, and pointing: "They tried to poison us! To kill us!"

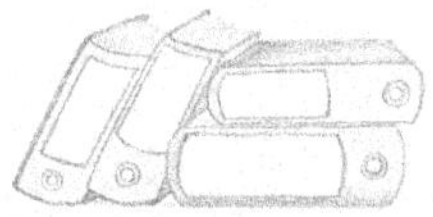

REMEMBER HOW YOU
LEARNED TO ACCEPT AND HANDLE
YOUR OWN POWER

Facilitators have no place in having an opinion about who should be in the room.

A key task of the facilitator is to enable participants to hold their own space without us, after they have left the space we've helped them to hold.

Our agenda and process are reflections of our own biases, preferences, assumptions and insecurities.

Sometimes, the sole purpose of a workshop is to find its purpose.

The only right and best way to facilitate is the one you choose in the very moment.

There is no how-to-guide for facilitation. Any other claim is deceiving.

An agenda is a deliberate deception into the predictability of a process.

The Facilitator's Creed for Guided Emergence

Emergence is the natural path of human interaction. Human interaction cannot be planned. Even within designed spaces, it finds its way to the surface.

Emergence is a highly vulnerable human dynamic wrapped in manifesting uncertainty. It reveals the actual needs, feelings, and desires behind every "I".

The most impactful transformation, experience, and learning process requires emergence at its core and cannot be pre-defined.

It requires is a space for people where things may emerge. Crafting this space is a fundamental intervention.

Process designs are counterintuitive to emergence, though they can be helpful if applied with the aim to create the emergent space.

Creating spaces for emergence comes with a high degree of responsibility. This responsibility must be earnt and honored.

Facilitating emergence is "applied diversity and inclusion". It allows for people to show up as themselves at any time.

Emergence can be stimulated or hampered,. Both are harmful.

While anything and everything can be used to facilitate emergence, words are helpful but are not essential. They can sometimes sabotage the objective.

It is crucial to offer guidance in the face of emergence. Guidance must always be an offer; is not a right, nor is it an order to be executed.

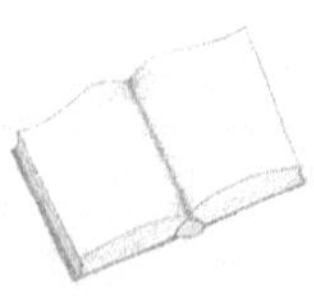

Presence makes up one part of the dynamic arising through emergence. Self-awareness is privileged at any moment.

A critical awareness of concerns with the unknown subconsciously limits my emergence in the group.

Hurdles must always be removed. Most preconceptions and insecurities are obstacles in the process.

Navigating emergent dynamics is the purest form of facilitation.

I AM ALLOWED TO KEEP FIVE OF MY SKILLS AS A FACILITATOR. THESE ARE THE FIVE AND THESE ARE THE REASONS WHY

Logistics before
instructions — always

MARK ON THIS DIAGRAM YOUR
RELATIONSHIP WITH AUTHORITY,
AS IT IS TODAY. ADD THE DATE FOR
FUTURE REFERENCE

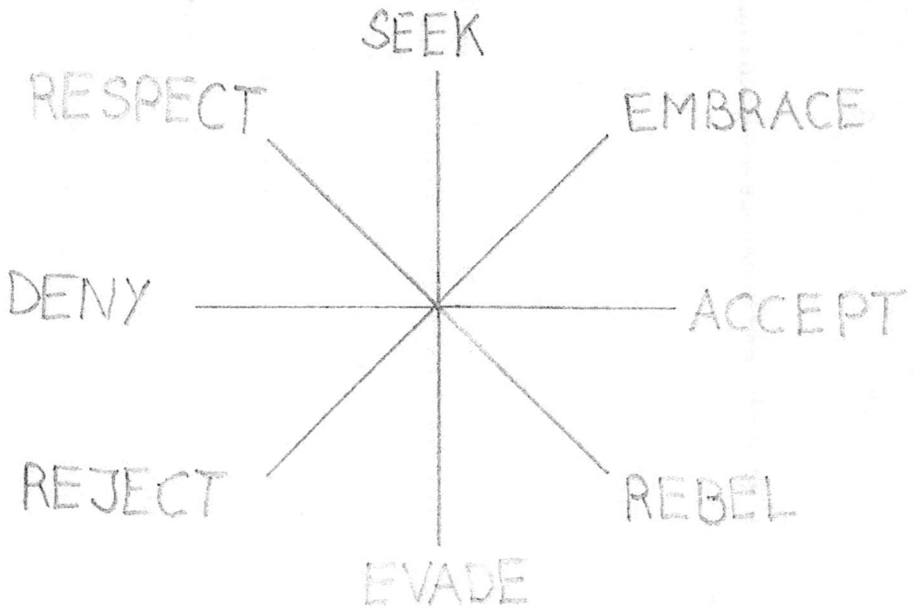

SEEK
RESPECT
EMBRACE
DENY
ACCEPT
REJECT
REBEL
EVADE

Facilitators who are blasé about an upcoming session are playing it safe, have accepted the assignment for the "wrong" reasons, are in a distracted mental state, need a break, or should consider doing something else for a living.

We must not believe human dynamics are unchanging just because they are recognizable.

Calling something "truth" will always lead to people getting defensive: they will claim more ownership and view other perspectives as threats.

We must never give up on anyone. Even if they say they don't want to be there. As long as they are, we can work with them.

A question is like a chameleon: it looks different depending on who asks, where, when, and how.

If you want the most revealing insights explore "why" frameworks don't work.

Over-instruction is a result of our own insecurity.

The algorithm to observe before inviting whoever we deem the most vulnerable to share: 1) be honest about whose need this is, and 2) make sure they are ready.

WRITE 500 WORDS ON
"WHAT YOU DO"
(IN YOUR PRACTICE).
TAKE A 10 MINUTE BREAK AND
EDIT THIS BY HALF. REPEAT UNTIL
YOU HAVE ONLY ONE SENTENCE OF
140 CHARACTERS LEFT

ILLOGICAL

We are approaching the end. I watch the trainer trying to land the intense and packed program she has guided us through, for days now. I can see her exhaustion, the struggle to maintain her high energy level and keep her patience in check.

She had been given the job of introducing the minutiae of a logical framework to a primarily Indigenous community. It was a donor requirement. I am beyond impressed with the participants' determination to work through this dry, foreign material at this energetic pace.

I catch myself almost nodding off during her final walk-through of all the walls plastered with flipcharts, boxes—a lot of boxes—and ideas for improving current projects. I count myself lucky for being an observer–advisor only, this time. She's still hanging in there.

"Are there any more questions?" she asks, wearily. A young man raises his hand. "Thank you so much for this exciting workshop. I understand now how the framework works. I am confused, however, by its name. Because there is absolutely nothing logical about it."

"What do you mean?" she says, astonished. "Logically, you move from box to box in a flow," she emphasises her response with angular, distinctive hand gestures. The young man waits politely for her to finish.

"I understand what you are saying. But there is nothing logical about it. Boxes have boundaries. And boundaries divide. They do not connect."

IDENTIFY THE ENERGY VAMPIRES IN YOUR PRACTICE. DRAW THEM, NAME THEM AND REVEAL THE WEAPON TO GET RID OF EACH ONE

whenyouinstructparticipants,youmustkeeptheessentialtoaminim
um.itisbestnottoaddextrawordsthatmightdiffuseyourmessage
becauseeachadditionalwordcreatesspaceforinterpretation.when
addressingthem,beconciseandtransparentinyourcommunication.
witheverywordyouriskcreatingbiases,steeringthegroupina
direction,andinfluencingeveryone'slearningjourney.itallstarts
withbeingclearaboutwhatyouwanttosayandwhyyouwantthemto
knowit.thisiscloselyconnectedtotheintentofwhatyoutellthem,
whichisrevealedthroughthechoiceofeverywordyouuse.usingtoo
manywordsalsoleadstoapotentiallossofattention.participants
finishtheinstructionsintheirheadsandareoftenalreadyengaged
intheircourseofactionbeforeyouhaveevenconcluded.withthe
instructionsbeingtooextensive,youoverreachyourmandateasa
facilitatorandinterferewiththenaturalexperience,whichcanleadto
furtherdeteriorationofengagementandfocus.whenyouplanyour
instructions,thinkaboutifthemessageisclear,andeasytocomprehend.
refrainfromtellingparticipantshowandwheretheycouldbeginor
fromgivingexamplesbecausethesewareallthingstheycanalways
discoverthemselves.whenyougivetoomuchawayintheinstructions,
itcanmakeparticipantsfeelalackofmasteryandrobsthemofthefull
potentialofanysituation,exercise,ortask.learningisaboutdiscovery;
ourwordscanturnawellintendedideaintoanegativelyremembered
duty…especiallywhenwedonotcarefullycraftourinstructions.
reduceyourinstructionsonlyto'what'andleavethe'why'.because
itofferspotentialforemergenttopics.revealingyourintentprime
stheparticipants.whenyouinstructinatoodetailedmanner,the
participantsarequicktofeelbelittledandpatronized,whichmight
adverselyaffecttheiracceptanceofyouintheroleoffacilitatorinthe
remainderofyourcollaboration,thusunderminingtheoverallprocess.
Instructtionsarebridgestolearningexperiences.don'tburnthem.

or:
Do not over-instruct.

Remember when
to simply shut up

CATCH THE TIME THIEVES
IN YOUR PRACTICE AND ARREST
EVERY SINGLE ONE

Reading the room is an individual approach to sense-making the dynamics around us.

In its essence, our role is about navigating human dynamics. "Just" that. And all of that.

Facilitation fatigue is a direct result of inefficiently acknowledging and addressing our emotional responses.

The chances of someone not liking what you do are infinitely higher than everyone liking what you do.

Facilitators are actors. Like actors, we bring our whole selves into the space and act according to the needs that we find there.

A facilitator who doesn't challenge is like a teacher who refuses to teach.

Agendas, if used, must to be a learning experience in itself, and never a standalone item.

There will always be more forms of facilitation than there are facilitators.

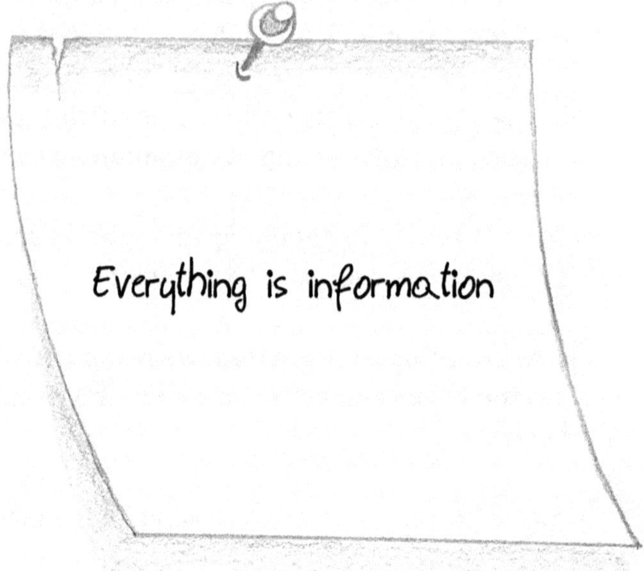
Everything is information

Those who give a one-dimensional answer that "I always enjoy my work" are either lying or in denial.

Instead of holding space, we should respect space, honor space and use space's generous opportunities through our interactions.

Regardless of the group, we must always learn "their language" quickly, without trying to hide "our accent".

Frameworks create an illusion of simplifying complexity.

Questions always induce, change or reinforce a power dynamic.

Before changing behavior, it is essential to uncover which purpose its continuation serves.

Frameworks are often used when human dynamics become too challenging to navigate, while this is exactly where they shouldn't be used.

THIS IS HOW I PERCEIVE I AM BEING PERCEIVED

SELF		OTHERS
	APPEARANCE	
	VALUES	
	BEHAVIOUR	
	ATTITUDE	

Being granted authority is an essential ingredient for facilitators to be able to act in the best interest of the participants.

There is never just one purpose. Our task is to make sure that collective and individual purposes can peacefully co-exist.

If we don't look closely, we might believe the participants' needs are theirs—when in fact they mirror ours.

Workshop, session, meeting, seminar, conference, training, sprint, retreat, off-site are just semantics. They all stand in for the same thing: a defined time in a given space where people interact.

Replacing neutral with impartial, all-partisan, non-partisan, just, fair or objective is meaningless. These are all subjectively assessed concepts.

We won't ever be able to avoid doing harm. We must never stop trying, regardless.

Inclusion is easy. It is how participants are included that makes all the difference.

Your inner helper needs to be monitored closely. And restrained.

WRITE DOWN YOUR SINGLE MOST IMPORTANT PIECE OF ADVICE FOR YOURSELF AND SHARE IT PUBLICLY

AUTHENTICITY

THINK OF A TIME WHERE YOU WERE AN AMAZING FACILITATOR, WRITE DOWN ALL THE REASONS WHY, AND CREATE A WALL OF SUCCESS. ONLY RULE: DON'T INCLUDE ANYTHING ATTRIBUTABLE TO THE PARTICIPANTS

Consciously applied tools and techniques are deliberate interferences with natural emergence.

No book, course, podcast or mentor will ever turn you into a facilitator. Only facilitating will.

The first step of handling power is to accept having it.

We seek raw, painful, challenging and honest experiences despite advertising them as fun, good times.

It is difficult to separate truth from "truths".

The moment we start thinking about being authentic we stop being our true selves.

Facilitation is not designing a process, it's navigating one.

If we talk about the group as having one identity, then there's no need for a facilitator.

MAKE A VOICE RECORDING OF AT LEAST 10 REASONS WHY SOMEONE SHOULD **NOT** BE FACILITATED BY YOU

CO-FACILITATION

WHEN DOES FACILITATION BEGIN AND WHEN DOES IT END?

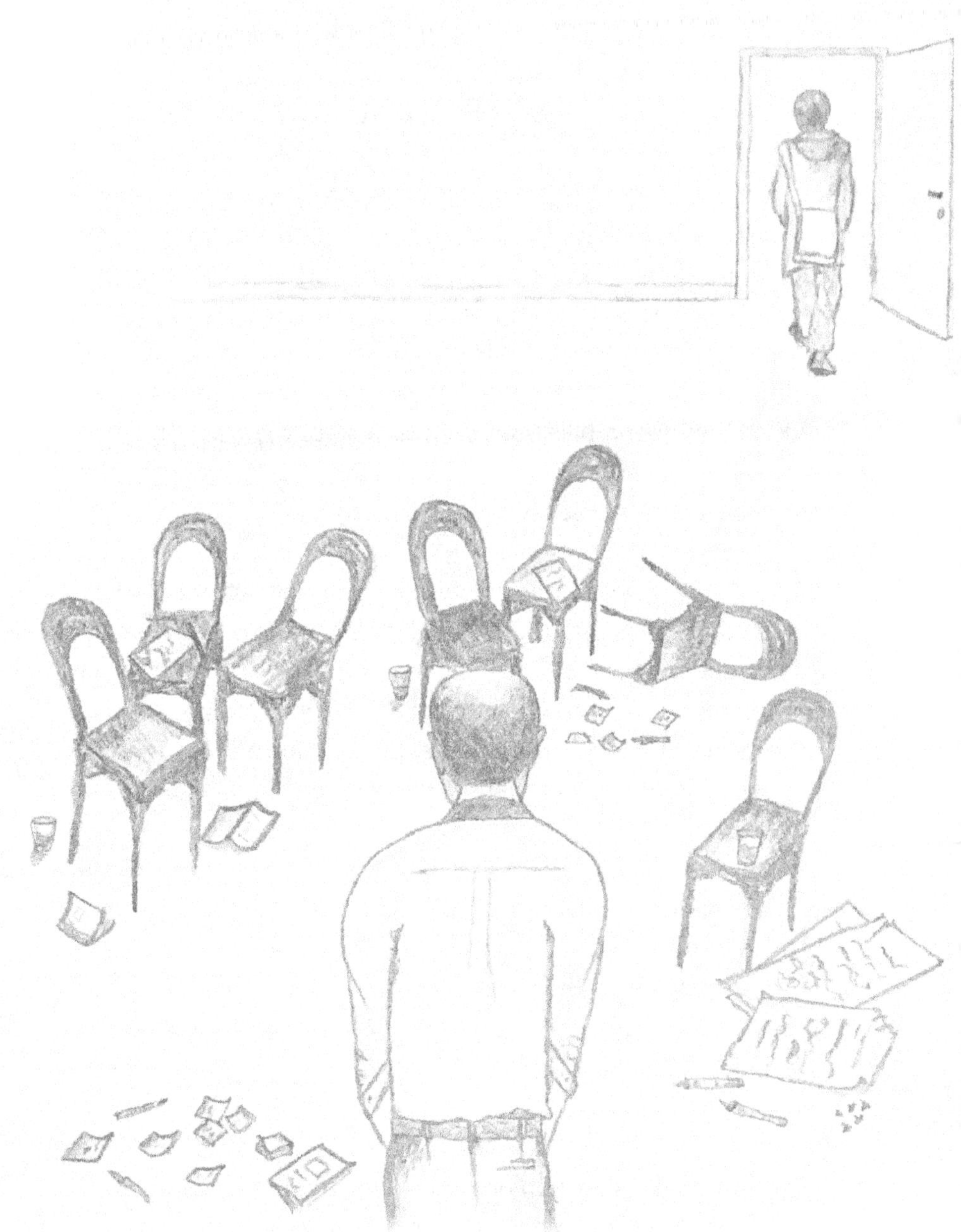

LONELINESS

STEP ASIDE

We are about to start. I am confident. Over-confident, really. A youth approaches me; he introduces himself, tells me he is 16, and that this is his first assignment as an interpreter. He tells me he sometimes works as a community facilitator for his peers in his village. His voice trembles slightly, and he wrings his hands. Today, he will be interpreting for respected elders. I tell him a bit about the purpose of the trust-building session and ensure him that I have complete confidence (and then some) that together, we will manage it.

When it is time, I am introduced as the guest of honor. This sort of intro is still jarring to me. I connect to the crowd of 50 or more men, women and children who have walked for over an hour in the heat to come to this gathering. They settle and all eyes are on me. I address the elders and introduce the day's purpose. As the young man translates, the mood changes in a moment.

Some jump up, screaming at me, and while I don't understand, their gestures are unmistakable. They are furious. My interpreter keeps calm and explains that they have already had several trust-building sessions. They are here to discuss the start of the project. This is the opposite of what I have been told.

I try to keep the situation under control, to pivot. I am not sure what the young man translates, but it seems to work. There is calm.

This might be good time to distribute refreshments. When I see bottled water being handed out, I notice, against my instruction, that someone has decided to include one pack of soda. Once all sodas have been distributed, the remaining elders refuse the water. They also want soda. When I tell them there is no more, frictions once more boil over. Screaming, accusations, and anger. I don't need an interpreter to understand that.

This shining young man of just 16 summers addresses them clearly—and without consulting with me. He calms everyone down once more.

Then he signals to me with a grave confidence: Step aside.

Every question can be formulated as a statement.

It is not what you do but how you do it that sets you apart.

Engagement has many faces.

If your only motive is to help others you are not being entirely honest to yourself.

Every single decision made in a workshop is non-neutral.

If helping isn't an offer, it becomes unwanted interference with the autonomy of the other.

Inclusion is method first, then result.

We don't serve the group, we support it.

REUNION

I am at the airport. One of the large ones that feels like what I imagine the inside of an anthill to be. People teeming. I have a layover before heading to an assignment in a conflict zone. I am already tired. I try to retreat and numb myself from the business around me. I am immersed in a bubble of my music, a carefully crafted playlist to help me detach from my surroundings, when I feel a careful touch on my shoulder.

I turn around to find myself face to face with a woman about my age. She seems somehow familiar. But I can't place her and I save myself the embarrassment of trying. I take off my headphones.

"Hi Thomas, I can't believe it." How warm and flushed my cheeks feel!

"Hi… I'm sorry, but I'm a bit lost now."

She laughs.

"No wonder! It must be ten years. I was in one of your workshops in South Africa."

Utterly baffled, I retrieve a vague memory of her, after hundreds, or even thousands of workshops since then.

"You remember me after all this time?"

"Of course. That workshop was a life-changer. This experience and watching you at work opened my eyes to a new career. I've been a trainer and facilitator for the last five years."

MAKE A VIDEO OF YOURSELF EXPLAINING HOW YOU TELL IF SOMEONE IS BEING AUTHENTIC

Transitions are the make-it or break-it of impactful facilitation.

Perfection is a decision, a mindset, a saboteur, and a choice. Not a result.

Facilitation is a like an artist painting in real time without the chance to change anything.

Normed ways of interaction are inauthentic by default.

Listening actively doesn't require saying anything.

Agendas are self-deceiving attempts to maintain control.

The benefits that come about from the effort of facilitation are impossible to measure.

GRAFFITI THIS PAGE WITH YOUR BIGGEST FEARS

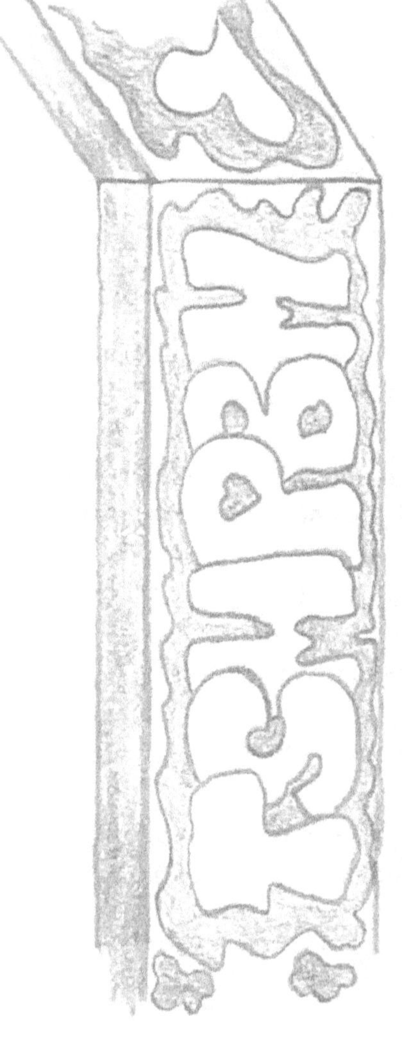

Fine lines

observation **is not the same as** recommendation

explanation **is not the same as** justification

honesty **is not the same as** transparency

co-creation **is not the same as** co-decision-making

authority **is not the same as** imposing

power **is not the same as** control

idea **is not the same as** solution

perspective **is not the same as** judgement

reality **are not the same as** truth

topics **is not the same as** people

listening **is not the same as** hearing

understanding **is not the same as** agreeing

curiosity **is not the same as** inquisition

harmony **is not the same as** psychological safety

connection **is not the same as** relationship

conflict avoidance **is not the same as** no conflict

responsibility **is not the same as** ownership

lonely **is not the same as** alone

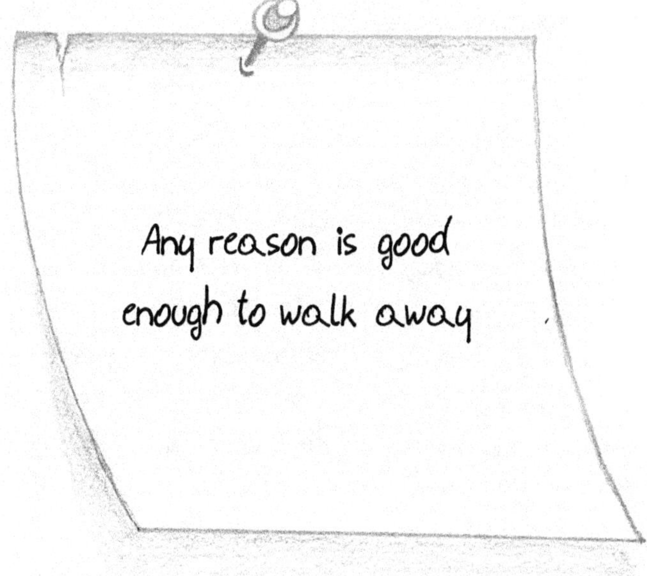
Any reason is good
enough to walk away

23 Theses on PS

1. Psychological safety is constantly fluid, temporal, and context dependent.

2. Psychological safety can never be experienced the same way from moment to moment.

3. Psychological safety is an undefined umbrella term that is experienced in a deeply subjective way. In other words, only individuals can define what psychological safety means for themselves.

4. Making our psychological safety dependent on others is disempowering; it undermines one's own power and relinquishes one's responsibility to oneself.

5. Psychological safety as a concept relies on the flawed assumption that the past predicts the future.

6. Psychological safety is never shared equally by everyone; by the way, it's unnecessary for everyone to feel the same.

7. Psychological safety is the confidence that my abilities and resources to handle the unknown threat are stronger than the threat I perceive.

8. The same system signalling confidence in one's ability to cope with any unkown threat undermines and enables psychological safety.

9. Facilitation is a temporary disruption. By default it is a threat to psychological safety.

10. Psychological safety is a technical term intending to reduce the experience of vulnerability.

11. Psychological safety can naturally evolve through contagion and role-modelling .

12. Facilitators regularly (sometimes subconsciously) fake psychological safety to role-model and encourage its evolution.

13. The success of a workshop is more dependent on participants embracing vulnerability than psychological safety .

14. Vulnerability and psychological safety are paradoxically connected. The more vulnerable our actions, the safer we feel. However, the safer we feel, the less vulnerable we perceive our actions to be.

15. Any session is an artificial setting. Experiencing psychological safety in such a setting is no guarantee that the sensation will last beyond it.

16. It is possible to experience different levels of safety within the same setting depending on the activity and constellation.

17. Psychological safety builds primarily on our own mental models, self-images, experiences, beliefs and assumptions. Not other people's behaviors.

18. Psychological safety is always about oneself and never about others. Others become projections or manifestations of our own insecurities.

19. Maintaining psychological safety over time requires continuous maintenance through honest self-reflection .

20. Power can be used as a catalyst for psychological safety.

21. Comparisons of all sorts are saboteurs of psychological safety. A collectively and continuously shared feeling of psychological safety is unachievable.

22. Dominating behavior and extroversion must never be mistaken for high levels of psychological safety.

23. Trust trumps psychological safety. I can trust everyone and still not feel safe, while the very lack of trust in anyone can lead to a form of safety.

TELL/WRITE
YOUR UNIQUE STORY AT LEAST
THREE DIFFERENT WAYS

You have come to the last page of the book!
This signals you to take the first step
of wherever you want to go next.

Before you go - thank you for accepting
my invitation!

Remember too: with every glance
you will find something new.

Now that you have taken a deep
look into that mirror, all that
remains is one final task:

go out and find someone to yorn
with.

Enjoy.

ACKNOWLEDGEMENTS

My family. This journey was the same as the first time: ups and downs, two steps forward, one step back, frustrations, excitement, doubts, and resilience. And you got all of it. All the time and on top of life happening. And while you involuntarily had to share my attention too many times, you remain my biggest cheerleaders and motivators. It doesn't go unnoticed and keeps me going. All my love.

Jane. There wouldn't be a book without you. When we first spoke about this, I don't think we both anticipated this roller coaster that was not only one of creativity but one of life's purest, most challenging, and most enjoyable surprises. You are truly a Jane of all trades and a master in each. I am eternally grateful for your guidance, your empathy, and for sharing your wisdom. The proudest result of all of this, however, is not this book. It is our friendship. The only question left: What are we up to next?

Hannah. I know you had no plan of doing this, and yet it's magic how you captured my journey and mental images so quickly and with such effortless precision. My appreciation for you and your dedication, passion, and creativity with which you adopted this book as yours exceeds any words. Before they were words on a page, your mind-blowing artwork made the book whole. Thank you for your patience with me.

Wolf. Thank you for your continued patience, determination, and flexibility. Your eye for detail and stoic smile when I wanted to change things for the umpteenth time served as an anchor. You might just be asked to do this again.

Steffi. You are just the most amazing little sister anyone can ask for. Oh, and the diagrams are perfect, but you knew that already.

Fellow facilitators and mentors. Your comments, practices, ideas, perspectives, and challenges have paved my way to self-awareness. While I am at a crossroads with an unknown destination, I will continue to sneak peek and get my dose of inspiration from time to time, and I will enjoy watching you continue on your respective paths. You all have my utmost respect and appreciation.

Every single participant. What I learned and will continue to learn from every one of you will remain invaluable. It took me these pages to understand the incredible privilege of being granted a facilitator mandate. It's a deep and fundamental trust in a human relationship that we don't value enough. I do now. Thank you—even though that feels pale and insufficient, I hope you know what I mean.

Thomas Lahnthaler is an international facilitator, mentor, author and speaker. He has collected two decades' in-depth experience from war zones to board rooms, and is known for his disruptive and thought-provoking approaches that challenge conventions. His work is heavily influenced by his time among Indigenous communities and his two greatest mentors, his children.

9 781739 628635